50 Japanese Grill Recipes for the Family

By: Kelly Johnson

Table of Contents

- Teriyaki Chicken
- Yakiniku (Japanese BBQ)
- Gyoza (Grilled Dumplings)
- Yakitori (Grilled Chicken Skewers)
- Miso-marinated Salmon
- Ebi (Grilled Shrimp)
- Tofu Steak
- Grilled Beef Tongue (Gyutan)
- Saba Shioyaki (Grilled Mackerel)
- Negima Yakitori (Chicken and Leek Skewers)
- Tori Katsu (Grilled Chicken Cutlets)
- Grilled Japanese Eggplant
- Grilled Squid (Ika)
- Unagi (Grilled Eel)
- Shishamo (Grilled Smelt)
- Grilled Vegetables (Nasu, Peppers, etc.)
- Robatayaki (Japanese Grilled Fish and Vegetables)
- Kushiage (Japanese Fried Skewers)
- Miso-glazed Pork Belly
- Grilled Japanese Sweet Potatoes
- Kakuni (Braised Pork Belly)
- Gindara Saikyo Yaki (Grilled Black Cod)
- Miso Grilled Scallops
- Grilled Japanese Corn with Soy Sauce
- Grilled Asparagus with Teriyaki Sauce
- Agedashi Tofu (Grilled Tofu in Soy Sauce)
- Grilled Sea Bass with Miso Marinade
- Hamachi Kama (Grilled Yellowtail Collar)
- Hōtō (Grilled Hotpot)
- Grilled Octopus (Tako)
- Gyu Kushi (Beef Skewers)
- Shioyaki (Salt-grilled Fish)
- Grilled Salmon Belly
- Grilled Mushrooms with Soy Sauce
- Grilled Shitake Mushrooms

- Charcoal-grilled Pork Ribs
- Grilled Zucchini with Sesame Dressing
- Grilled Takoyaki (Octopus Balls)
- Grilled Dango (Sweet Rice Dumplings)
- Soy Sauce Marinated Grilled Chicken Thighs
- Japanese Grilled Shrimp with Garlic Butter
- Grilled Tofu with Teriyaki Sauce
- Grilled Tuna Steaks with Wasabi
- Karrage (Japanese Fried Chicken)
- Grilled Avocado with Soy Sauce
- Miso Grilled Aubergine (Eggplant)
- Grilled Japanese Hot Dogs
- Grilled Hamachi (Yellowtail) Steaks
- Sautéed Grilled Vegetables with Teriyaki Sauce
- Grilled Beef Rib Eye Steak with Wasabi

Teriyaki Chicken

Ingredients:

- **Chicken thighs** (boneless, skinless)
- **Soy sauce**
- **Mirin**
- **Sake**
- **Sugar**
- **Garlic** (minced)
- **Ginger** (grated)
- **Sesame seeds** (for garnish)

Instructions:

1. **Make the Teriyaki Sauce:**

    - In a small saucepan, combine soy sauce, mirin, sake, sugar, garlic, and ginger. Simmer for 10-15 minutes until the sauce thickens.

2. **Cook the Chicken:**

    - Heat a pan or grill over medium heat. Cook the chicken thighs until golden brown on both sides and cooked through.

3. **Glaze the Chicken:**

    - During the last few minutes of cooking, brush the chicken with the teriyaki sauce, allowing it to caramelize.

4. **Serve:**

    - Slice the chicken and serve with rice, garnished with sesame seeds and additional sauce.

Yakiniku (Japanese BBQ)

Ingredients:

- **Beef** (sirloin, ribeye, or short ribs, thinly sliced)
- **Soy sauce**
- **Mirin**
- **Sake**
- **Sugar**
- **Garlic** (minced)
- **Sesame oil**

Instructions:

1. **Make the Marinade:**
   - In a bowl, combine soy sauce, mirin, sake, sugar, garlic, and sesame oil. Mix well.
2. **Marinate the Beef:**
   - Place the sliced beef in the marinade and let it sit for at least 30 minutes.
3. **Grill the Beef:**
   - Preheat the grill or a hot griddle. Grill the beef slices for 2-3 minutes per side until cooked to your desired doneness.
4. **Serve:**
   - Serve with steamed rice and dipping sauce.

Gyoza (Grilled Dumplings)

Ingredients:

- **Ground pork** (or chicken)
- **Cabbage** (finely chopped)
- **Garlic** (minced)
- **Ginger** (minced)
- **Green onions** (chopped)
- **Soy sauce**
- **Sesame oil**
- **Gyoza wrappers**

Instructions:

1. **Make the Filling:**

    - In a bowl, combine ground pork, cabbage, garlic, ginger, green onions, soy sauce, and sesame oil. Mix well.

2. **Form the Dumplings:**

    - Place a spoonful of the filling in the center of each gyoza wrapper. Fold and pleat the edges to seal.

3. **Grill the Dumplings:**

    - Heat oil in a skillet over medium heat. Place the dumplings in the pan and cook until the bottoms are golden brown. Add a little water to steam and cook the tops.

4. **Serve:**

    - Serve with a dipping sauce made from soy sauce and rice vinegar.

Yakitori (Grilled Chicken Skewers)

Ingredients:

- **Chicken thighs** (cut into bite-sized pieces)
- **Green onions** (cut into 2-inch pieces)
- **Soy sauce**
- **Mirin**
- **Sake**
- **Sugar**
- **Sesame oil**
- **Skewers** (wooden or metal)

Instructions:

1. **Make the Sauce:**

    - In a saucepan, combine soy sauce, mirin, sake, sugar, and sesame oil. Simmer for 10-15 minutes until thickened.

2. **Prepare the Skewers:**

    - Thread chicken and green onion pieces alternately onto the skewers.

3. **Grill the Skewers:**

    - Preheat the grill. Grill the skewers, brushing with the yakitori sauce, until the chicken is cooked through and slightly charred.

4. **Serve:**

    - Serve hot with steamed rice.

Miso-marinated Salmon

Ingredients:

- **Salmon fillets**
- **Miso paste** (white or red)
- **Mirin**
- **Sake**
- **Sugar**

Instructions:

1. **Make the Marinade:**
    - In a bowl, combine miso paste, mirin, sake, and sugar. Mix well.
2. **Marinate the Salmon:**
    - Coat the salmon fillets with the miso marinade and refrigerate for at least 30 minutes.
3. **Grill or Bake the Salmon:**
    - Preheat the grill or oven. Grill or bake the salmon for 10-12 minutes or until cooked through.
4. **Serve:**
    - Serve with steamed rice and vegetables.

Ebi (Grilled Shrimp)

Ingredients:

- **Shrimp** (peeled and deveined)
- **Soy sauce**
- **Lemon juice**
- **Garlic** (minced)
- **Sesame oil**

Instructions:

1. **Marinate the Shrimp:**

    - In a bowl, combine soy sauce, lemon juice, garlic, and sesame oil. Add the shrimp and marinate for 10-15 minutes.

2. **Grill the Shrimp:**

    - Preheat the grill. Thread the shrimp onto skewers and grill for 2-3 minutes per side until pink and cooked through.

3. **Serve:**

    - Serve the shrimp with rice or as a topping for noodles.

Tofu Steak

Ingredients:

- **Firm tofu** (cut into thick slices)
- **Soy sauce**
- **Sesame oil**
- **Garlic** (minced)
- **Green onions** (for garnish)

Instructions:

1. **Prepare the Tofu:**
    - Press the tofu to remove excess moisture. Slice into thick pieces.
2. **Marinate the Tofu:**
    - In a bowl, mix soy sauce, sesame oil, and garlic. Marinate the tofu slices for at least 10 minutes.
3. **Cook the Tofu:**
    - Heat oil in a pan. Fry the tofu slices until golden brown on both sides.
4. **Serve:**
    - Serve with steamed rice, garnished with green onions.

Grilled Beef Tongue (Gyutan)

Ingredients:

- **Beef tongue** (sliced)
- **Soy sauce**
- **Sake**
- **Mirin**
- **Garlic** (minced)
- **Sesame oil**

Instructions:

1. **Prepare the Marinade:**
    - In a bowl, combine soy sauce, sake, mirin, garlic, and sesame oil.
2. **Marinate the Beef Tongue:**
    - Marinate the beef tongue slices for at least 30 minutes.
3. **Grill the Beef Tongue:**
    - Preheat the grill and cook the beef tongue slices for 2-3 minutes on each side.
4. **Serve:**
    - Serve with steamed rice and a dipping sauce.

Saba Shioyaki (Grilled Mackerel)

Ingredients:

- **Mackerel fillets**
- **Salt**
- **Lemon** (for garnish)

Instructions:

1. **Salt the Mackerel:**

    - Sprinkle the mackerel fillets with salt and let them sit for 10 minutes.
2. **Grill the Mackerel:**

    - Preheat the grill. Grill the mackerel for 4-5 minutes per side, or until the skin is crispy and the fish is cooked through.
3. **Serve:**

    - Serve with rice and a slice of lemon.

Negima Yakitori (Chicken and Leek Skewers)

Ingredients:

- **Chicken thighs** (cut into bite-sized pieces)
- **Leeks** (cut into 2-inch pieces)
- **Soy sauce**
- **Mirin**
- **Sake**
- **Sugar**

Instructions:

1. **Make the Sauce:**
    - In a saucepan, combine soy sauce, mirin, sake, and sugar. Simmer until thickened.
2. **Prepare the Skewers:**
    - Thread the chicken and leek pieces onto the skewers alternately.
3. **Grill the Skewers:**
    - Grill the skewers, brushing with the sauce, until the chicken is cooked through and charred.
4. **Serve:**
    - Serve the skewers hot with steamed rice.

Tori Katsu (Grilled Chicken Cutlets)

Ingredients:

- **Chicken breasts** (boneless, skinless)
- **Soy sauce**
- **Mirin**
- **Sake**
- **Garlic** (minced)
- **Ginger** (grated)
- **Panko breadcrumbs**
- **Egg** (beaten)
- **Flour**
- **Sesame oil**

Instructions:

1. **Prepare the Marinade:**
   - In a bowl, combine soy sauce, mirin, sake, garlic, and ginger. Marinate the chicken breasts for 20-30 minutes.
2. **Bread the Chicken:**
   - Dredge the marinated chicken in flour, dip in the beaten egg, and coat with panko breadcrumbs.
3. **Grill the Chicken:**
   - Heat sesame oil in a pan or on the grill. Cook the chicken cutlets until golden brown and cooked through, about 5-6 minutes per side.
4. **Serve:**
   - Serve with steamed rice and tonkatsu sauce for dipping.

Grilled Japanese Eggplant

Ingredients:

- **Japanese eggplant** (sliced lengthwise)
- **Soy sauce**
- **Mirin**
- **Sesame oil**
- **Garlic** (minced)
- **Green onions** (for garnish)
- **Sesame seeds** (for garnish)

Instructions:

1. **Prepare the Marinade:**
    - In a bowl, combine soy sauce, mirin, sesame oil, and garlic.
2. **Grill the Eggplant:**
    - Brush the eggplant slices with the marinade and grill over medium heat for 3-4 minutes per side until tender.
3. **Serve:**
    - Garnish with chopped green onions and sesame seeds before serving.

Grilled Squid (Ika)

Ingredients:

- **Whole squid**
- **Soy sauce**
- **Sake**
- **Mirin**
- **Lemon juice**
- **Garlic** (minced)
- **Sesame oil**

Instructions:

1. **Prepare the Squid:**

    - Clean the squid, removing the tentacles and inner parts. Score the body of the squid in a criss-cross pattern.

2. **Make the Marinade:**

    - In a bowl, combine soy sauce, sake, mirin, lemon juice, garlic, and sesame oil. Marinate the squid for 15-20 minutes.

3. **Grill the Squid:**

    - Preheat the grill and cook the squid for about 2-3 minutes per side until lightly charred and cooked through.

4. **Serve:**

    - Serve with a sprinkle of sesame seeds and lemon wedges.

Unagi (Grilled Eel)

Ingredients:

- **Unagi (eel fillet)** (fresh or thawed)
- **Soy sauce**
- **Mirin**
- **Sake**
- **Sugar**
- **Garlic** (optional)
- **Rice vinegar**

Instructions:

1. **Prepare the Sauce:**

    - In a saucepan, combine soy sauce, mirin, sake, sugar, and a splash of rice vinegar. Simmer for 15 minutes to create a glaze.

2. **Grill the Eel:**

    - Preheat the grill. Brush the eel fillet with the glaze and grill for 5-7 minutes, brushing with more glaze during cooking.

3. **Serve:**

    - Serve the eel over steamed rice, garnished with additional glaze.

Shishamo (Grilled Smelt)

Ingredients:

- Shishamo (smelt fish)
- Soy sauce
- Mirin
- Sake
- Sugar

Instructions:

1. **Make the Marinade:**

    - In a bowl, mix soy sauce, mirin, sake, and sugar. Marinate the smelt fish for 10-15 minutes.

2. **Grill the Fish:**

    - Preheat the grill and cook the smelt fish for 2-3 minutes per side, until lightly crispy and cooked through.

3. **Serve:**

    - Serve with rice or as a side dish, garnished with sesame seeds.

Grilled Vegetables (Nasu, Peppers, etc.)

Ingredients:

- **Japanese eggplant** (Nasu), bell peppers, zucchini, and mushrooms
- **Soy sauce**
- **Mirin**
- **Sesame oil**
- **Garlic** (minced)
- **Green onions** (for garnish)

Instructions:

1. **Prepare the Marinade:**

    - Combine soy sauce, mirin, sesame oil, and minced garlic in a bowl.

2. **Marinate the Vegetables:**

    - Slice the vegetables and marinate them in the mixture for 15-20 minutes.

3. **Grill the Vegetables:**

    - Preheat the grill. Grill the vegetables for 3-4 minutes per side until tender and lightly charred.

4. **Serve:**

    - Garnish with chopped green onions and sesame seeds before serving.

Robatayaki (Japanese Grilled Fish and Vegetables)

Ingredients:

- **Assorted fish** (salmon, mackerel, etc.)
- **Assorted vegetables** (shiitake mushrooms, asparagus, bell peppers)
- **Soy sauce**
- **Mirin**
- **Sake**
- **Sesame oil**
- **Garlic** (minced)

Instructions:

1. **Make the Marinade:**

    - In a bowl, combine soy sauce, mirin, sake, sesame oil, and garlic.
2. **Marinate the Fish and Vegetables:**

    - Marinate the fish fillets and vegetables in the mixture for 15-30 minutes.
3. **Grill the Ingredients:**

    - Preheat the grill. Grill the fish and vegetables, basting with the marinade, until cooked through.
4. **Serve:**

    - Serve the grilled fish and vegetables on skewers, with dipping sauce if desired.

Kushiage (Japanese Fried Skewers)

Ingredients:

- **Chicken, shrimp, vegetables** (carrots, zucchini, mushrooms, etc.)
- **Panko breadcrumbs**
- **Egg** (beaten)
- **Flour**
- **Soy sauce**
- **Mirin**
- **Vegetable oil** (for frying)

Instructions:

1. **Prepare the Ingredients:**

    - Thread the chicken, shrimp, and vegetables onto skewers.
2. **Bread the Skewers:**

    - Dredge the skewers in flour, dip in the beaten egg, and coat in panko breadcrumbs.
3. **Fry the Skewers:**

    - Heat oil in a frying pan or deep fryer. Fry the skewers for 3-4 minutes or until golden brown.
4. **Serve:**

    - Serve with a dipping sauce made from soy sauce and mirin.

Miso-glazed Pork Belly

Ingredients:

- **Pork belly** (sliced into pieces)
- **Miso paste** (red or white)
- **Soy sauce**
- **Mirin**
- **Sugar**
- **Garlic** (minced)
- **Sesame oil**

Instructions:

1. **Make the Miso Glaze:**

    - In a bowl, combine miso paste, soy sauce, mirin, sugar, garlic, and sesame oil. Stir well.

2. **Marinate the Pork Belly:**

    - Coat the pork belly slices with the miso glaze and marinate for 1 hour.

3. **Grill the Pork Belly:**

    - Preheat the grill and cook the pork belly slices for 4-5 minutes per side until caramelized and cooked through.

4. **Serve:**

    - Serve with steamed rice and vegetables.

Grilled Japanese Sweet Potatoes

Ingredients:

- **Japanese sweet potatoes** (Satsumaimo)
- **Olive oil** or **Sesame oil**
- **Sea salt**
- **Cinnamon** (optional)

Instructions:

1. **Prepare the Sweet Potatoes:**

    - Wash the sweet potatoes thoroughly and cut them into thick slices or wedges.

2. **Grill the Sweet Potatoes:**

    - Brush the sweet potatoes with olive oil or sesame oil. Season with sea salt and a sprinkle of cinnamon if desired.
    - Grill over medium heat for 20-25 minutes, turning occasionally, until they are tender and lightly charred.

3. **Serve:**

    - Serve as a side dish or a snack.

Kakuni (Braised Pork Belly)

Ingredients:

- **Pork belly** (cut into cubes)
- **Soy sauce**
- **Mirin**
- **Sake**
- **Sugar**
- **Ginger** (sliced)
- **Garlic** (crushed)
- **Green onions** (for garnish)

Instructions:

1. **Prepare the Pork Belly:**
    - Heat a pan over medium heat and sear the pork belly cubes until golden brown on all sides.
2. **Braise the Pork Belly:**
    - Add soy sauce, mirin, sake, sugar, ginger, and garlic. Add enough water to cover the pork belly. Bring to a simmer.
    - Cover and braise for 1.5-2 hours until the pork is tender and the sauce has thickened.
3. **Serve:**
    - Garnish with chopped green onions and serve with rice.

Gindara Saikyo Yaki (Grilled Black Cod)

Ingredients:

- **Black cod fillets**
- **Saikyo miso** (sweet white miso)
- **Sake**
- **Mirin**
- **Sugar**
- **Soy sauce**

Instructions:

1. **Prepare the Marinade:**

    - Mix saikyo miso, sake, mirin, sugar, and soy sauce in a bowl.
2. **Marinate the Cod:**

    - Coat the black cod fillets in the marinade and refrigerate for 4-6 hours or overnight.
3. **Grill the Cod:**

    - Preheat the grill and cook the cod fillets for about 5-7 minutes per side, until golden and caramelized.
4. **Serve:**

    - Serve with steamed rice and a side of vegetables.

Miso Grilled Scallops

Ingredients:

- **Scallops** (fresh, shells removed)
- **White miso paste**
- **Soy sauce**
- **Mirin**
- **Sake**
- **Sesame oil**
- **Green onions** (for garnish)

Instructions:

1. **Prepare the Miso Marinade:**
    - Mix white miso paste, soy sauce, mirin, sake, and sesame oil in a bowl.
2. **Marinate the Scallops:**
    - Coat the scallops with the marinade and let them sit for 10-15 minutes.
3. **Grill the Scallops:**
    - Preheat the grill to medium heat and cook the scallops for 2-3 minutes per side until they are just cooked through.
4. **Serve:**
    - Garnish with chopped green onions and serve with rice or as an appetizer.

Grilled Japanese Corn with Soy Sauce

Ingredients:

- **Japanese corn** (or regular corn on the cob)
- **Soy sauce**
- **Butter**
- **Sugar**

Instructions:

1. **Prepare the Corn:**

    - Husk the corn and grill it over medium heat for 10-12 minutes, turning occasionally, until charred and cooked through.

2. **Glaze the Corn:**

    - In a small bowl, mix soy sauce, butter, and sugar. Brush the mixture onto the corn during the last few minutes of grilling.

3. **Serve:**

    - Serve the corn with extra glaze for dipping.

Grilled Asparagus with Teriyaki Sauce

Ingredients:

- **Asparagus** (trimmed)
- **Teriyaki sauce**
- **Sesame oil**

Instructions:

1. **Prepare the Asparagus:**

    - Toss the asparagus with sesame oil and season with a pinch of salt.//
2. **Grill the Asparagus:**

    - Grill the asparagus over medium heat for 5-7 minutes until tender and lightly charred.
3. **Add Teriyaki Sauce:**

    - Brush with teriyaki sauce during the last minute of grilling.
4. **Serve:**

    - Serve as a side dish with your favorite protein.

Agedashi Tofu (Grilled Tofu in Soy Sauce)

Ingredients:

- **Firm tofu** (cut into cubes)
- **Soy sauce**
- **Mirin**
- **Sake**
- **Cornstarch** (for coating)
- **Vegetable oil** (for frying)
- **Bonito flakes** (optional)

Instructions:

1. **Prepare the Tofu:**

    - Drain and press the tofu to remove excess moisture. Cut into cubes.
2. **Coat the Tofu:**

    - Lightly dust the tofu cubes with cornstarch.
3. **Grill or Fry the Tofu:**

    - Heat vegetable oil in a pan and fry the tofu cubes until golden and crispy on all sides, about 4-5 minutes.
4. **Prepare the Sauce:**

    - In a small bowl, combine soy sauce, mirin, and sake. Heat the mixture in a saucepan for 2-3 minutes.
5. **Serve:**

    - Pour the sauce over the tofu and garnish with bonito flakes, if desired.

Grilled Sea Bass with Miso Marinade

Ingredients:

- Sea bass fillets
- White miso paste
- Soy sauce
- Mirin
- Sake
- Honey

Instructions:

1. **Make the Marinade:**

    - In a bowl, mix white miso paste, soy sauce, mirin, sake, and honey.

2. **Marinate the Sea Bass:**

    - Coat the sea bass fillets with the marinade and let them sit for 30 minutes to 1 hour.

3. **Grill the Sea Bass:**

    - Preheat the grill and cook the fillets for 3-4 minutes per side until golden brown and cooked through.

4. **Serve:**

    - Serve with rice and sautéed vegetables.

Hamachi Kama (Grilled Yellowtail Collar)

Ingredients:

- **Yellowtail collar** (Hamachi Kama)
- **Soy sauce**
- **Lemon juice**
- **Sake**
- **Sesame oil**
- **Green onions** (for garnish)

Instructions:

1. **Prepare the Marinade:**

    - In a bowl, combine soy sauce, lemon juice, sake, and sesame oil.

2. **Marinate the Collar:**

    - Coat the yellowtail collar in the marinade and refrigerate for 20-30 minutes.

3. **Grill the Collar:**

    - Preheat the grill and cook the yellowtail collar for 5-7 minutes per side until golden and crispy.

4. **Serve:**

    - Garnish with chopped green onions and serve with rice.

Hōtō (Grilled Hotpot)

Ingredients:

- **Beef or pork slices**
- **Tofu**
- **Mushrooms** (shiitake, enoki, etc.)
- **Pumpkin** (sliced)
- **Noodles** (flat wheat noodles)
- **Soy sauce**
- **Sake**
- **Mirin**
- **Dashi stock**
- **Green onions** (for garnish)

Instructions:

1. **Prepare the Hotpot Ingredients:**

    - Slice the beef or pork, tofu, mushrooms, and pumpkin. Cook the noodles separately.

2. **Make the Soup Base:**

    - In a large pot, combine dashi stock, soy sauce, sake, and mirin. Bring to a simmer.

3. **Grill and Assemble:**

    - Grill the meat, tofu, and vegetables separately on skewers or in a grill pan.
    - Add the grilled items to the hotpot and simmer together with the cooked noodles for 5-10 minutes.

4. **Serve:**

    - Serve hot, garnished with green onions.

Grilled Octopus (Tako)

Ingredients:

- **Octopus tentacles**
- **Soy sauce**
- **Mirin**
- **Sake**
- **Lemon juice**
- **Garlic** (crushed)
- **Olive oil**
- **Sesame seeds** (for garnish)

Instructions:

1. **Prepare the Octopus:**
   - Boil the octopus tentacles for 45 minutes or until tender. Drain and let them cool.
2. **Make the Marinade:**
   - In a bowl, mix soy sauce, mirin, sake, lemon juice, and garlic. Coat the octopus in the marinade and let it sit for 30 minutes.
3. **Grill the Octopus:**
   - Preheat the grill to medium-high. Grill the octopus tentacles for 2-3 minutes on each side until lightly charred.
4. **Serve:**
   - Garnish with sesame seeds and serve with a side of rice or vegetables.

Gyu Kushi (Beef Skewers)

Ingredients:

- **Beef sirloin or tenderloin** (cut into bite-sized cubes)
- **Soy sauce**
- **Mirin**
- **Sake**
- **Sugar**
- **Garlic** (minced)
- **Green onions** (for garnish)
- **Wooden skewers**

Instructions:

1. **Prepare the Marinade:**
   - Mix soy sauce, mirin, sake, sugar, and garlic in a bowl.
2. **Marinate the Beef:**
   - Thread the beef cubes onto wooden skewers and marinate them in the sauce for 30-60 minutes.
3. **Grill the Skewers:**
   - Preheat the grill and cook the beef skewers for 2-3 minutes per side, until desired doneness.
4. **Serve:**
   - Garnish with chopped green onions and serve.

Shioyaki (Salt-grilled Fish)

Ingredients:

- **Whole fish** (such as mackerel, sea bream, or trout)
- **Sea salt**
- **Lemon wedges** (optional)

Instructions:

1. **Prepare the Fish:**

    - Clean and gut the fish, leaving the scales on for grilling. Pat the fish dry.
2. **Salt the Fish:**

    - Generously rub sea salt over the fish, inside and out. Let it rest for 10-15 minutes.
3. **Grill the Fish:**

    - Preheat the grill and cook the fish for 5-7 minutes per side, depending on the size, until crispy and fully cooked.
4. **Serve:**

    - Serve with lemon wedges for squeezing on top.

Grilled Salmon Belly

Ingredients:

- Salmon belly slices
- Soy sauce
- Mirin
- Sake
- Brown sugar
- Lemon juice

Instructions:

1. **Prepare the Marinade:**

    - Mix soy sauce, mirin, sake, brown sugar, and lemon juice in a bowl.
2. **Marinate the Salmon:**

    - Coat the salmon belly slices with the marinade and let them sit for 20-30 minutes.
3. **Grill the Salmon:**

    - Preheat the grill and cook the salmon belly for 3-4 minutes per side until golden and crispy.
4. **Serve:**

    - Serve with steamed rice or vegetables.

Grilled Mushrooms with Soy Sauce

Ingredients:

- **Mixed mushrooms** (shiitake, enoki, oyster, etc.)
- **Soy sauce**
- **Sesame oil**
- **Garlic** (minced)
- **Green onions** (for garnish)
- **Sesame seeds** (for garnish)

Instructions:

1. **Prepare the Mushrooms:**

   - Clean and slice the mushrooms. If using large mushrooms, cut them into halves or quarters.

2. **Marinate the Mushrooms:**

   - Mix soy sauce, sesame oil, and minced garlic. Toss the mushrooms in the marinade and let them sit for 10 minutes.

3. **Grill the Mushrooms:**

   - Preheat the grill and cook the mushrooms for 5-7 minutes, turning occasionally, until tender and slightly charred.

4. **Serve:**

   - Garnish with chopped green onions and sesame seeds.

Grilled Shitake Mushrooms

Ingredients:

- **Shiitake mushrooms** (stemmed)
- **Soy sauce**
- **Mirin**
- **Sesame oil**
- **Garlic** (minced)

Instructions:

1. **Marinate the Mushrooms:**

    - Mix soy sauce, mirin, sesame oil, and minced garlic in a bowl. Toss the shiitake mushrooms in the marinade and let them sit for 15 minutes.

2. **Grill the Mushrooms:**

    - Preheat the grill and cook the shiitake mushrooms for 3-5 minutes on each side until soft and smoky.

3. **Serve:**

    - Serve as a side dish or appetizer.

Charcoal-grilled Pork Ribs

Ingredients:

- **Pork ribs**
- **Soy sauce**
- **Honey**
- **Garlic** (minced)
- **Ginger** (grated)
- **Rice vinegar**
- **Five-spice powder**

Instructions:

1. **Prepare the Marinade:**

    - In a bowl, mix soy sauce, honey, garlic, ginger, rice vinegar, and five-spice powder.

2. **Marinate the Ribs:**

    - Coat the pork ribs in the marinade and refrigerate for 4 hours or overnight.

3. **Grill the Ribs:**

    - Preheat the grill to medium-low. Grill the ribs for 2-3 hours, turning occasionally, until tender and caramelized.

4. **Serve:**

    - Slice the ribs and serve with grilled vegetables or rice.

Grilled Zucchini with Sesame Dressing

Ingredients:

- **Zucchini** (sliced into rounds or strips)
- **Sesame oil**
- **Soy sauce**
- **Rice vinegar**
- **Honey**
- **Sesame seeds**

Instructions:

1. **Grill the Zucchini:**
    - Brush the zucchini slices with sesame oil and grill over medium heat for 3-5 minutes per side until tender.
2. **Prepare the Dressing:**
    - In a bowl, mix soy sauce, rice vinegar, and honey.
3. **Serve:**
    - Drizzle the dressing over the grilled zucchini and garnish with sesame seeds.

Grilled Takoyaki (Octopus Balls)

Ingredients:

- **Takoyaki batter** (flour, dashi stock, egg, baking powder, etc.)
- **Octopus chunks**
- **Tempura scraps**
- **Pickled ginger**
- **Soy sauce**
- **Takoyaki sauce**
- **Bonito flakes**

Instructions:

1. **Prepare the Takoyaki:**

   - Make the takoyaki batter using flour, dashi, egg, and baking powder. Pour the batter into a takoyaki grill pan and add chunks of octopus, tempura scraps, and pickled ginger to each hole.

2. **Grill the Takoyaki:**

   - Turn the takoyaki balls using a skewer until golden and crispy on the outside, about 4-5 minutes.

3. **Serve:**

   - Drizzle with takoyaki sauce, soy sauce, and sprinkle with bonito flakes.

Grilled Dango (Sweet Rice Dumplings)

Ingredients:

- Glutinous rice flour
- Sugar
- Water
- Soy sauce
- Mirin
- Rice vinegar

Instructions:

1. **Make the Dango Dough:**

    - Mix glutinous rice flour, sugar, and water to form a smooth dough. Roll the dough into small balls.

2. **Grill the Dango:**

    - Thread the dango balls onto skewers and grill for 5-7 minutes, turning occasionally until golden.

3. **Prepare the Sauce:**

    - Mix soy sauce, mirin, and rice vinegar in a small saucepan and simmer until thickened.

4. **Serve:**

    - Brush the dango with the sauce and serve.

Soy Sauce Marinated Grilled Chicken Thighs

Ingredients:

- **Chicken thighs** (bone-in or boneless)
- **Soy sauce**
- **Honey**
- **Garlic** (minced)
- **Ginger** (grated)
- **Rice vinegar**
- **Sesame oil**

Instructions:

1. **Make the Marinade:**

   - Combine soy sauce, honey, garlic, ginger, rice vinegar, and sesame oil in a bowl.

2. **Marinate the Chicken:**

   - Coat the chicken thighs in the marinade and refrigerate for at least 1 hour.

3. **Grill the Chicken:**

   - Preheat the grill to medium-high and cook the chicken thighs for 6-8 minutes per side until golden and fully cooked.

4. **Serve:**

   - Serve with steamed rice and a side of grilled vegetables.

Japanese Grilled Shrimp with Garlic Butter

Ingredients:

- **Shrimp** (peeled and deveined)
- **Butter**
- **Garlic** (minced)
- **Soy sauce**
- **Lemon juice**
- **Parsley** (chopped)
- **Lemon wedges** (for garnish)

Instructions:

1. **Prepare the Shrimp:**

    - Toss the shrimp in soy sauce and lemon juice, then set aside for 10-15 minutes to marinate.

2. **Make the Garlic Butter:**

    - In a pan, melt butter over medium heat, add minced garlic, and sauté for 1-2 minutes until fragrant.

3. **Grill the Shrimp:**

    - Preheat the grill. Grill shrimp for 2-3 minutes per side, until they turn pink and opaque.

4. **Serve:**

    - Drizzle the garlic butter over the grilled shrimp and garnish with chopped parsley and lemon wedges.

Grilled Tofu with Teriyaki Sauce

Ingredients:

- **Firm tofu** (pressed and cut into thick slices)
- **Teriyaki sauce**
- **Sesame oil**
- **Green onions** (for garnish)
- **Sesame seeds** (optional)

Instructions:

1. **Marinate the Tofu:**

    - Coat the tofu slices in teriyaki sauce and let them marinate for 30 minutes.
2. **Grill the Tofu:**

    - Preheat the grill and lightly oil the grill grates. Grill the tofu for 3-4 minutes per side, until grill marks appear and the tofu is golden.
3. **Serve:**

    - Drizzle with additional teriyaki sauce and garnish with chopped green onions and sesame seeds.

Grilled Tuna Steaks with Wasabi

Ingredients:

- Tuna steaks
- Soy sauce
- Olive oil
- Wasabi paste
- Lemon juice
- Black pepper

Instructions:

1. **Prepare the Marinade:**
    - Mix soy sauce, olive oil, lemon juice, and black pepper in a bowl.
2. **Marinate the Tuna:**
    - Coat the tuna steaks in the marinade and refrigerate for 15-20 minutes.
3. **Grill the Tuna:**
    - Preheat the grill to medium-high. Grill the tuna steaks for 2-3 minutes per side for medium-rare or longer for your desired doneness.
4. **Serve:**
    - Serve with a dollop of wasabi paste and a squeeze of lemon juice.

Karrage (Japanese Fried Chicken)

Ingredients:

- **Chicken thighs** (boneless, skinless, cut into bite-sized pieces)
- **Soy sauce**
- **Ginger** (grated)
- **Garlic** (minced)
- **Cornstarch**
- **All-purpose flour**
- **Salt** and **pepper**
- **Vegetable oil** (for frying)
- **Lemon wedges** (for garnish)

Instructions:

1. **Marinate the Chicken:**

    - Combine soy sauce, ginger, garlic, salt, and pepper in a bowl. Add the chicken and marinate for 30 minutes.

2. **Prepare the Coating:**

    - Mix cornstarch and flour in a bowl. Dredge the marinated chicken in the flour mixture.

3. **Fry the Chicken:**

    - Heat vegetable oil in a deep pan to 350°F (175°C). Fry the chicken pieces for 4-6 minutes until golden and crispy.

4. **Serve:**

    - Serve with lemon wedges on the side.

Grilled Avocado with Soy Sauce

Ingredients:

- **Avocados** (cut in half and pitted)
- **Soy sauce**
- **Sesame oil**
- **Lime juice**
- **Sesame seeds** (optional)
- **Chili flakes** (optional)

Instructions:

1. **Prepare the Avocados:**

    - Brush the flesh of the avocado halves with sesame oil and grill cut-side down for 2-3 minutes until grill marks appear.

2. **Serve:**

    - Drizzle with soy sauce, lime juice, and a sprinkle of sesame seeds and chili flakes, if desired.

Miso Grilled Aubergine (Eggplant)

Ingredients:

- **Eggplant** (cut into thick slices)
- **Miso paste** (white or red)
- **Soy sauce**
- **Honey** or **sugar**
- **Sesame oil**
- **Green onions** (for garnish)

Instructions:

1. **Prepare the Miso Glaze:**
    - In a bowl, combine miso paste, soy sauce, honey, and sesame oil.
2. **Grill the Aubergine:**
    - Preheat the grill and brush the eggplant slices with the miso glaze. Grill for 4-5 minutes per side until soft and lightly charred.
3. **Serve:**
    - Garnish with chopped green onions and serve.

Grilled Japanese Hot Dogs

Ingredients:

- **Japanese-style hot dog sausages** (or regular hot dogs)
- **Buns**
- **Wasabi mayo** (optional)
- **Pickled ginger** (optional)

Instructions:

1. **Grill the Hot Dogs:**
   - Preheat the grill and grill the hot dogs for 3-4 minutes, turning occasionally, until golden and crispy.
2. **Serve:**
   - Place the grilled hot dogs in buns, and top with wasabi mayo and pickled ginger if desired.

Grilled Hamachi (Yellowtail) Steaks

Ingredients:

- **Hamachi steaks** (yellowtail)
- **Soy sauce**
- **Mirin**
- **Lemon juice**
- **Black pepper**

Instructions:

1. **Prepare the Marinade:**

    - Mix soy sauce, mirin, lemon juice, and black pepper in a bowl.
2. **Marinate the Hamachi:**

    - Coat the hamachi steaks in the marinade and refrigerate for 20-30 minutes.
3. **Grill the Hamachi:**

    - Preheat the grill to medium-high. Grill the hamachi steaks for 2-3 minutes per side until cooked through.
4. **Serve:**

    - Serve with steamed rice or a salad.

Sautéed Grilled Vegetables with Teriyaki Sauce

Ingredients:

- **Mixed vegetables** (zucchini, bell peppers, mushrooms, asparagus, etc.)
- **Soy sauce**
- **Mirin**
- **Sesame oil**
- **Garlic** (minced)
- **Sesame seeds** (for garnish)

Instructions:

1. **Grill the Vegetables:**

    - Preheat the grill and lightly oil the grill grates. Grill the vegetables for 3-4 minutes per side until tender and slightly charred.

2. **Prepare the Teriyaki Sauce:**

    - In a saucepan, combine soy sauce, mirin, sesame oil, and minced garlic. Simmer for 2-3 minutes.

3. **Sauté the Vegetables:**

    - Toss the grilled vegetables in the teriyaki sauce and sauté for another 2 minutes.

4. **Serve:**

    - Garnish with sesame seeds and serve.

Grilled Beef Rib Eye Steak with Wasabi

Ingredients:

- **Rib-eye steak**
- **Soy sauce**
- **Wasabi paste**
- **Garlic** (minced)
- **Olive oil**
- **Black pepper**

Instructions:

1. **Marinate the Steak:**

    - Mix soy sauce, wasabi paste, garlic, olive oil, and black pepper in a bowl. Coat the steak in the marinade and let it sit for 30 minutes.

2. **Grill the Steak:**

    - Preheat the grill to medium-high. Grill the steak for 4-5 minutes per side for medium-rare or longer for desired doneness.

3. **Serve:**

    - Serve the steak with a side of wasabi for an extra kick.